Emily

by Beate Sigriddaughter

Emily

by Beate Sigriddaughter

EMILY
Copyright©2020 Beate Sigriddaughter
All Rights Reserved
Published by Unsolicited Press
Printed in the United States of America.
First Edition.

All rights reserved. Printed in the United States of America. No part of this book may be used or reproduced in any manner whatsoever without written permission except in the case of brief quotations embodied in critical articles or reviews.

Attention schools and businesses: for discounted copies on large orders, please contact the publisher directly.

For information contact:
Unsolicited Press
Portland, Oregon
www.unsolicitedpress.com
orders@unsolicitedpress.com
619-354-8005

Cover Design: Kathryn Gerhardt
Editor: S.R. Stewart

ISBN: 978-1-950730-22-3

Poems

MORNING	2
REBEL TRAINING	4
MOTHER SUNDAY MORNING	5
BEAUTY	7
SOLITUDE	8
SARTRE BY THE RIVER	9
A CHALLENGED SOUL	10
16TH STREET MALL SHUTTLE	12
POWER	13
THE LOOK	14
ON ICE	15
EMILY WATCHES HER HUSBAND BRING KATE A GLASS OF WATER	17
BACKPACK	19
EMILY WATCHES HIM SHARPEN KITCHEN KNIVES	20
EMILY'S LETTER TO HER HUSBAND'S LOVER	21
A ROSE IN PARIS	23
FOREST FIRE	24
HE DANCED WELL	25
DESIRE	26
EMILY CELEBRATES HER INSIGNIFICANCE	27
EMILY WRITES TO HER FATHER IN HEAVEN	28

RED SCARF	30
PINK SLIP	31
GRAY	32
ROSEMARY HONEY	33
WHILE SHE WAS DANCING	34
WORK	35
WHY SHE IS IN LOVE AGAIN	36
ON HER CLIMB TO GRATITUDE	37

Emily

MORNING

Early
times of wild
anticipation, each
waking an event,
eyes open to surprises,
sunrise, sudden
excellence
of toes or hair
or even green skies
bold in paintings,
the quivering
wait after lunch
of bread soup,
for finally night
so old-fashioned
candles on the tree
could be lit. Christmas
Eve magic, days
she was not jealous
yet of things
she didn't even want
she was still
good enough for life.

Long before she knew
how to dance
she knew it was coming.

She longs to wake again
to wander in snow,
reunited with her breathless
elfin adoration.

REBEL TRAINING

There are people born without rebellion,
gliding lovely through their days, taking
your breath away, golden, like sunrise
sliding over the morning's mountain.
She was not one of them.

It started early. How could God
waste all these children that lived
unbaptized, lost because
their villages had never heard of Him?

Lately she read contemporary human beings
have an attention span of eight seconds
which is less than the attention span
of a goldfish. She wondered how
do you measure a goldfish attention span.

A while back she read it cost the state
a hundred thousand dollars to rehabilitate
one rapist. She wondered who would pay
as much for rehabilitation of his prey.

And so discomfort darkened
her protective mantle of rebellion
over wanting to love almost everything.

MOTHER SUNDAY MORNING

It is usually like this. She endures
her husband's volatile search
for cufflinks. She finds them
on the windowsill, hands them
over to a grudging grunt
of thanks. She dons her hat,
her pride, light brown felt
with a dark brown velvet band.
To her it is the ultimate
in elegance. They walk to church.
She is so pleased with her hat
which, unlike a man, she gets
to wear throughout the service
which has now begun, a baritone
insulting women from the pulpit
as is so often the case. Eve's sin,
lust and lascivious temptations,
et cetera. She no longer hears.
Her mind has taken off, it floats
now over the flowers at the altar,
larkspur and white roses on white
lace, the flicker of candle light,
a sunray through transparent glass
casts magic mist on everything.
Cool white marble underfoot.
Dust dances in the light. She drifts
over how young she was once,
children close by, even the one
killed in the war. Now the choir

sings. She wants to keep this
forever. This is her time
to sit and soar in private beauty.

BEAUTY

If it were
a green stone,
she would pick it
for its beauty.
It was a wad
of chewing gum.
She passed.

SOLITUDE

Grandmother loved her
solitude, to read, for instance,
even when the sun was out, yes,
even in lovely May.
Emily's mother didn't much like her.
They'd had sundry fallings out
over perceived insults, especially
when grandmother proclaimed,
accurately and injudiciously, how
you could always get another wife,
but never another mother.

Emily would have preferred
to play by herself in the garden,
or do something with her friends.
Her brothers, too, had other
preferences. Nonetheless, each
Sunday afternoon they all went
to visit grandmother who would
rather have read at home alone.

They walked together in the park.
None of them wanted to be there.
All thought it was their duty.
All were mildly angry, bored.
And this was how they loved
and tormented each other
with helpless excellent intentions.

SARTRE BY THE RIVER

Emily sees her former self read Sartre
by the river on a misty Sunday morning.
Nobody, she believes, knows where she is,
what she is doing. Her parents think
she went to church, she thinks,
to the late morning sermon, her hymnal
in her baggy red purse instead of
Being and Nothingness of which
she doesn't understand a word, even
in translation. No matter. The title,
lovely, certainly intrigues. She wants
to say no to something without hurting
anyone. And so her life begins
with secrets and the scent of grass,
ducks on the water, words on the page,
wind in her problematic hair.

A CHALLENGED SOUL

When she was ten, she had a glowing
moment of nobility. Anyone who asked
for anything at all, she resolved,
if she had it, she would give it.
How her young soul shimmered.

First test came at eleven, summer camp.
A zealous fellow camper asked
for contributions to a worthy cause.
Emily can't remember what it was.
Bangladesh, Africa, something to do
with children and hunger most likely.
She had made plans already
for her small allowance, had felt rich,
expansive. She canceled plans and gave
what she had. She did not suffer exactly,
but forever after she disliked the girl
for asking.

These days she takes a shortcut
through back alleys on her way to work.
She walks by broken bottles,
two or three times a mattress
labeled "bedbugs" by the dumpster
pungent with fish and other things.
This to avoid the sidewalk out front,
next to the Lutheran church

where a heavy man sits each morning
asking for spare change in exchange
for a smiling *God Bless.*

Her soul feels dusty and defensive.

16TH STREET MALL SHUTTLE

On the way home from riding the roller coaster
twice, once in the front car, still fizzy with thrill,
Emily sits down on the mall shuttle, then notices
a small black man, even older than she is,
standing, leaning on a cane. All other seats
are taken. She jumps up and offers him her seat.
"No, thanks," he says with a wrinkled smile,
"but you could give me a blow job.
Do something that's really useful." She turns
her head. Above them a sign reads
"Cancer cures smoking."

POWER

The man at the traffic light
trips her and she falls on the ground.
He bends over her, unfolds a pocket knife,
shows her the miniscule blade, grins,
and stretches out his hand to help her up.
In disbelief she takes his hand and stands.
He walks away.

THE LOOK

He stands at the water's edge,
looks at bald eagles circling overhead.
Two at first, then three, then four.
He looks in silence and he looks
with longing. Somewhere up there
in those circles he is looking for his soul.
The sun magnificently pierces
dense white clouds.

She blows on her gloved knuckles
to warm them through the wool.
He used to look at her like that.

ON ICE

Every woman wants a volunteer
in love, someone who wants to give
her pleasure even as she lets him off
the hook. So Emily, for example, one
New Year's Eve at the ice rink:
They'd made a date two weeks before.
He didn't seem particularly enthusiastic,
so she said, *If you don't want to, I'll go
by myself.* She never thought
he would accept and opt to sit nearby
in a café to read a magazine, while she
rented her skates and entered the rink.
The music was sweet, the lights
were magic as she skated round
and round, gliding among children
who seemed far more experienced
than she was. Light was laced
with laughter. Blue turned pink, purple.
She hardly noticed. Hope kept
throbbing, a strobe light in her brain.
Any minute now he would appear
with sudden skates on his feet,
laughing as they cautiously held hands,
imitating champions with attempts
at grace, then quickly grabbing a gate
or a post or a railing for balance.
Once she thought she saw his ponytail.
She was mistaken. In the second hour
she made peace with the amazing

gap in her chest, a shrine for hope,
even for a half hour, a quarter.
Then time was up. A fanfare,
a wish for a Happy New Year.
Did you enjoy yourself? he asked.
She considered lying. Then she said, *No.*

EMILY WATCHES HER HUSBAND BRING KATE A GLASS OF WATER

Kate has lovely skin
the color of hazelnut. Her hair is rich
and long. Her dark eyes sparkle
youth, longing, confidence.
The left corner of her lips
lifts with imperious amusement.

Emily, considerably older, remembers
a former husband mention once:
*What makes a woman beautiful is
the promise of sex. It doesn't have to be
fulfilled. The promise is enough.*

Several men hum around Kate
in a dance that displays
their beauty, their strength, their
captivated veneration.

Now Emily watches her husband
bring Kate a glass of water.
Kate acknowledges with a nod
and open eyes of surprised
appreciation.

Emily's husband told her once:
*What makes a woman desirable
is a certain air of helplessness.*

Emily shivers helplessly
in her brave strength and competence.

BACKPACK

She always imagined
she would die at thirty-six.
That turned out to be
the year she married.

Her husband hated dancing
with older women.
One morning she woke up
and realized
she was an older woman.

Rummaging in the crawl space,
she noticed her green backpack
was older than her husband's girlfriend.

EMILY WATCHES HIM SHARPEN KITCHEN KNIVES

Rust red stone, water, patience.
A thin pitched sound repeats
as steel glides to perfection.
She wishes one could sharpen love
like that to trim the dull
fat of acceptance and complacency.

EMILY'S LETTER TO HER HUSBAND'S LOVER

*Sometimes I suffer still
from envy of things I don't want.
It feels like defeat. Truth, like a glacial mirror,
shimmers with reality. Are you, perhaps,
the lucky one whose portion of desire
will not dim with use?*

*You know things. You gave him a pool cue
as a gift where I'm not even sure how to spell it.*

*There was a time I dreamed of making love
each day. Soon scent and music were left out.
Desire wilted on the windowsill
while he still tried to soothe me
with his ice-cold hands of generous indifference.
Today—this feels like progress—I don't envy
you this roller coaster ride, this steep ascent
of open-mouthed anticipation, then
the gentling to a shaky stop.*

*I slip the curtain from each morning, step
into the sunlight of regret. I almost kept him
on the shelf with all the trophies. He doesn't belong
there, though my ego keens
about the empty space.*

*I am grateful I had fire once, a wedding
night, a single sequin on a velvet gown.
I do not want to have my edges dulled
or his. I imagine you together,
he freshly showered, his eyes drip warmth.
Perhaps you can keep desire alive.
I yearn for my own season of hunger.*

A ROSE IN PARIS

Emily was so worthless once,
after scrimping and saving
so they could both go to Paris
for his conference and drink
café au lait in the basement
breakfast room of their hotel
(not the conference hotel
which cost considerably more)
and then walk rainy streets,
when they passed a flower shop
window with white roses
on display and he asked
"Do you want me to buy you a rose?"
she said, *"Er, no."*
He was so clueless once,
had he just said, "wait a minute,"
entered the shop and come back
with a rose, she would have been
ecstatic, never mind the expense.
But she was worthless then.
Things are better now. They travel
separately in the world, although
she has never forgotten that rose.

FOREST FIRE

There were ashes on her soul
and she felt the death of things
that was going to come their way.
She wanted to be close to him
so that when death finally arrived
they would be together at least
with the beat of the other one's heart
and their eyes locked in love
saying good-bye gently,
with the ashes gray against
the windshield, like gray snow
dusting the heart,
and the acrid bite in the air,
the sun orange with warning:
Look, you aren't forever.
She felt a soft murmur of fear
in fiery gloom, wind blowing
fine ash again and again.
A little later their love burned out,
leaving black satin skeletons of trees.

HE DANCED WELL

He told her how she was
his destiny, had been so since,
oh, before the beginning of time.
He told his next wife how
she was meaningless to him,
which this next wife in turn
apologetically reported back
in a moment of fierce ache,
but not until after she too
had been replaced by
an even younger woman.
Emily, quite happy by then,
found it hard to sort out
which was more hurtful,
to have been meaningless
or to hear it reported to her.
Presumably he tells his youngest
wife enchanting stories now.
He always danced well
and probably still does.

DESIRE

Emily stands surrounded by glitter,
typical temptations, silk fabric,
color threads, rhinestones, beads,
and she wants none of them today.
She considers some hand soap
enticingly called "unicorn tears."
Even that leaves her cold. In the end
she doesn't even want to dance tonight.
Is this enlightenment? she wonders.
If so, she doesn't want it. All
she wants is her desire back,
slick and lovely hum of yearning.

EMILY CELEBRATES HER INSIGNIFICANCE

Rocks, seals, or driftwood
down below. She cannot tell.
A garland of sleek cormorants
glides low above the water.

This is where life has spit her
with its froth of insignificance.

If she weren't so insignificant,
she would have important duties
elsewhere, stand on a stage,
perhaps, or cater to a love.

Poppies and rattlesnakes, otters,
once even a fox. Life is.

EMILY WRITES TO HER FATHER IN HEAVEN

Dear Dad,

*It is dark autumn. I remember
your dramatic whispers on New Year's Eve,
your hand cupped over your left ear:
"The year slinks away. Listen.
Can you hear it?" I listen
to gypsy music often these days, still
wanting to find that one song you used
to sing in the car. It is a haunting tune,
words full of tears of love or longing,
I can't remember which. I remember
your vibrant baritone. I know
how to play the melody on my flute,
but haven't been able to find the song
in everyday reality.*

*I know you wanted to be loved. You did
all you could to make this happen,
and I truly wanted to comply
and love. It simply never came to pass.
There was a barrier between us,
your occasional rage, my cautious mistrust
of you, your God, your Nazi past. You went
to Heaven fourteen years ago. I know
you went to Heaven. That was always*

*the plan. I never cried for you. At first
I waited for the tears to come.
After a few years I stopped waiting.*

*I have hundreds of pages of notes
about you, more than I had
for my dissertation before I decided
to drop out of school. I am bewildered
here. If I cannot love you, how can I
ever be good enough for life and how
can life be good enough for me?*

RED SCARF

Emily in winter wears a bright red scarf,
a contrast to the snow, skating to Christmas music
at the ice rink by the National Gallery of Art
for instance, or hiking, scarf lilting happily
on icy trails along the Gila Wilderness.

She visited a loved one once, and his new wife
who made him so at long last happy
it made Emily happy too. They sipped hot cider
together and window shopped downtown
in breezy wind. Suddenly he said, *pick something
to remember us, for instance a cashmere pashmina shawl.*
Emily reached for the bright red, yes. For once
she knew exactly what she wanted.

That's not a good color for you, his new wife declared.
It doesn't flatter your complexion. Must have read
a book about complementary colors. For Emily
she picked discreet pale green sage blossom beige,
as Emily's hand reluctantly withdrew from the red.
Trust me, she said. The scarf hangs in Emily's closet,
costly, and well-preserved. Yes, Emily remembers them,
their classy well-meaning, posh pashmina,
while she conducts her happiest days in red
microfiber bought for five dollars at Walmart.

It might not flatter her complexion,
but it goes well with her soul.

PINK SLIP

Emily stands by the window, contemplating
life. A former colleague comes to mind, Jolene,
who didn't go an extra inch, never mind mile,
but used her spare time to gossip, criticize
both equals and superiors, and on occasion
to compose chain prayers for ailing friends
from church. The layoffs started. Suddenly
an email from Jolene to all: *I have some
time. Does anyone need help?* It was too late.
The next round swept her away.

Outside a child laughs. A woman's voice,
impatient, scolds. The laughter fades.
Emily's hands tremble on the pink letter
from radiology. It mentions changes
that require more evaluation. *I love you,
world,* she whispers. *You are good
enough for me.* She hopes it isn't too late.

GRAY

At forty-seven, Emily stopped coloring
her hair to dance-floor platinum.
She wanted to witness her first gray.
She waited and waited. Then one day
the fluorescent office restroom light
hit two of her hairs just so. Yes. Gray.
She tried to cry. It wasn't convincing,
even to herself. Also, there was much
left to do to earn her living. Papers
to be filed, things to be typed.

She didn't feel the least bit different,
a little lonelier than usual perhaps.
Nobody cared if she cried or not.
She understood what she had
always known: Even for her
there would be no exception.

Sometime later politics
made everything irrelevant.
It no longer mattered if her belly
was flabby or her hair turned gray.
All that mattered was the fear in her
unsettled bowels.

In autumn on the trail she noticed
even asters had gray hair.

ROSEMARY HONEY

A man just stomped on her
last sliver of interest
in a desperately friendly gathering
by blistering her words
with expert self-absorption.

It is not just contempt she feels,
but boredom, emptiness, as hungry
ghosts circle around the potluck spread,
picking up an olive of applause,
a grape of mild wrath, a crumb
of visibility, a boastful morsel
of consideration of the moment.

A woman looks at her with starving
eyes. She can tell they have nothing
in common. Somehow, they must
survive. *Someone said you brought
this honey,* Emily says. *Oh yes,*
the woman eagerly responds. Her eyes
relax. *It's rosemary honey. We also
brought cheeses from upstate New York.
Try some. They go together well.*

WHILE SHE WAS DANCING

While she was dancing tango one Sunday
night, cheek-to-cheek with friendly strangers,
shots rang out elsewhere. Fifty-nine futures
were stolen, many more wounded,
including her own, by an invisible rage
that declared thou shalt not dance or laugh
in paradise.

She learned their many names to chant them
down into the sands of time, while dreaming
still of a world of peace and dance for all.

While she was running by the ocean,
she felt the death of thousands of children
starved, diseased, unnamed, and unrecorded,
fading from lack of importance. She is starving
for a ray of sanity beneath a sun
that could so easily support them all.

WORK

Duty is a form of suicide.
It murders from within.
When she works for a boss
for money, nobody bothers
to ask for her time.

But when she works for herself
she feels guilty. She does
not listen to her best friend's pain,
does not make love to her lover,
does not cook or visit relatives.
She is guilty of preferring
her life to reality.

WHY SHE IS IN LOVE AGAIN

Because
he drove back to show her
a snake on the road
she had missed. He herded it
off into forest grass.
That's when they noticed
its dead mate curled
at the edge of the pavement.
Minutes later he drove back
again to move the dead one,
too—*still soft*, he said,
with recent life—in case
the living snake returned
for its mate and had better not
lie in the middle of traffic.

ON HER CLIMB TO GRATITUDE

On her steep climb to gratitude,
impatient as ever, she stumbles, twists
her ankle, limps into a whisper
of God's breath: *I only want to be
honored. I too dislike critique,
my friend, I don't want to be told
what to do or when. Trust me, I know
what I am doing. This world is my best
shot.* Not once did God declare
I am too good for you. She feels
the loud black wings of ravens beat
as though they were her own.
How beautiful you are, she sings.

Acknowledgments

Thank you to the editors of the following publications where some of these poems first appeared, some in slightly different form:

Blue Fifth Review: "The Look"
Chiron Review: "Forest Fire"
Cultural Weekly: "Emily Watches Her Husband Bring Kate a Glass of Water"
Figroot Press: "Sartre By the River"
Five 2 One Magazine: "Backpack"
Gargoyle: "On Ice," Emily Watches Him Sharpen Kitchen Knives," "Rosemary Honey"
Literati Magazine: "16th Street Mall Shuttle," "Emily Writes to Her Father in Heaven," "A Challenged Soul"
Mad Swirl: "Morning," "Beauty"
Scarlet Leaf Review: "Power"
Silver City Quarterly Review: "Emily Celebrates Her Insignificance," "While She Was Dancing"
Sin Fronteras: "Red Scarf"
Thirteen Myna Birds: "Pink Slip"
Voices on the Wind: "He Danced Well," "Gray," "On Her Climb to Gratitude"
The Write Place at the Write Time: "Why She Is in Love Again"

Many thanks to Dale Rucklos for building my writing space and Michael Schulte for sponsoring it, to Ann Hedlund for providing me a retreat space near the ocean where many of these poems were first envisioned, and to

Jaxon Burgess who expertly keeps my laptop in good working shape.

With deepest gratitude to Michael Schulte who choreographs my happiness so that my words may dance.

About the Author

Beate Sigriddaughter, www.sigriddaughter.net, was poet laureate of Silver City, NM (Land of Enchantment) from 2017 – 2019. She grew up in Nürnberg, Germany, where she began her trajectory of enchantment a five-minute walk from the castle. Alternate playgrounds, even closer to home, were World War II bomb ruins. Contrasts in her life became the norm. Her writing has received multiple Pushcart Prize nominations and a handful of poetry prizes. Keenly interested in women and their situation in the world, she created the blog *Writing In A Woman's Voice* where she publishes other women's work.

About the Press

Unsolicited Press is a small press in Portland, Oregon. The progressive publishing house was founded in 2012 by editors who desired a stronger connection with writers. The team publishes award-winning fiction, poetry, and creative nonfiction.

Learn more at www.unsolicitedpress.com.

www.ingramcontent.com/pod-product-compliance
Lightning Source LLC
Chambersburg PA
CBHW030135100526
44591CB00009B/663